lithium

bipolar poetry

yogesh chandra

ISBN: 978-982-98178-3-9

Writers Contact details: yogeshchandra1994@gmail.com
Website: https://writerscornerfiji.wixsite.com/poetryandfiction

Also by Yogesh Chandra
The Tragedy of our Lives
A Beautiful Poison
The Flower that Went Mad
The Words I Could Never Say

out of all the pills i took,
the one that made some
difference in my life was
the one i overdosed on.

-irony

this is for you: the silent cries that you've become so used to…

it's the middle of the night, and the sad silvery sheet is the only thing left for you to hold onto. with the tightest of grips, you lie face down, gently applying more pressure as your cries get louder. by this stage, you can taste the abundant, sweet tears that have started flowing uncontrollably. and then, the sudden realization: you had just wept a few hours ago.

the seconds pass by unhurriedly as your thoughts slowly become disordered and shapeless. to your left, attached to the wall, is a big bold note you wrote to yourself some days ago, reminding you to *"never end your life, no matter what"*. you have a quick, deafening stare but feel nothing. your mind has once again started to traverse the land of an instantaneous, painless *end* to everything you're going through. after all, it's the only thing making sense to you at this hour.

the cries grow louder, and with it, the compulsion to just do it right this time. so you get up, pick up the slender knotted rope, and put it around your sunburnt soft neck. there is a brief pause as you scramble to write just one more note. *"i was once happy"*, you start inking. there is a short but thoughtful silence all around the room as you slowly utter: *"what am i even doing?"*

it is at this moment that you decide to continue holding onto the greatest gift of all: life. these long and dreadfully cold nights haven't magically gone away, but you have come to the realization that you never had before: life has to be lived no matter what.

today, as you sit under the radiant yellow sun, you're taken back to that night. what if you had decided to just let go?

well, for one, you'd not be reading this right now. and the many things you'd never get to feel—ever. life is a rollercoaster of ups and downs. realizing that everything is temporary could be a great start. most importantly, i'm glad that you decided to not give up. i'm so proud of you—truly.

contents

7

as i take my next breath,
i'm confronted with the
grim reality:

i have already written my
suicide note a few weeks
ago.

-only the depressed die

you left my heart in pieces. so i had
to pick each one up, painstakingly
stitch them together, and pretend
that everything was alright.

but, at times, the thread breaks and
leaves me with a fresher wound.

-i still can't get over you

9

we are both in pain, my love.

the only thing different about
us is that you will get to live.

-the suicidal mind

and so, pill after pill, i lay there
effortlessly swallowing—quiet,
numb, and almost losing count.
patiently waiting for the misery
to stop.

-overdose

11

the words you spoke when
we first met was undeniably
magical.

but it was the last few where
poetry started.

-heartbreak

yogesh chandra

the reason why one of us is
happy and the other is not:

we both asked for happiness
from the same place.

-shortage of smiles

13

everyone wants the prettiest
flowers from the garden, but
no one ever thinks:

it's the same petals that have
seen love turn into heartbreak.

-the reason why flowers don't talk

today, i felt a little creative, so
ended up scribbling some
poetry.

last week i did too, but ended
up writing a suicide note.

-the bipolar brain

15

i wrote you a song, pointed it
to the moon, and asked her to
sing it to you. but the moon
came back and told me that it
had already been sung to you.

just not from me.

-my first heartbreak

i forgot to water the flowers
for a week, and soon they
wilted. but what's tragic is
that they did not complain
for a bit.

even while dying.

-caring too much about others

lithium

17

i sunk to my lowest,
day by day.

but in the end, it was
you who shed all the
tears.

-on my funeral

18

every night, i blankly stare at the
high and impenetrable wall right
next to me.

and at times, happen to notice
the note i so concernedly wrote
to myself some years ago—on
a *good* day.

[please never end your life yogesh...]

and if magically, i was given the chance
to change just one event of my past, i'd
perhaps:

get papa to still be here, or prevent all
my childhood trauma, or skip through
my first heartbreak, or undo the times
i've hurt my mother, or not think about
ending my life every single day, or not
push away the people closest to me, or
stop overthinking at every beat of the
heart, or stop all the self-doubt each time
i wanted to do something new, or not
get a complete breakdown each time
someone was unkind to me, or stop all
the tears from falling every time i felt
vulnerable.

i'd perhaps choose the easiest of all:

not be born.

-i vs i

i cried in the rain, thinking
that no one would notice.
but i had forgotten:

the cloud above me was
also crying.

-the weeping games

21

you asked me how i was doing.
i smiled and replied, *"not very
well."* so you said you'd bring
some flowers to cheer me up.
the next day, flowers you did.

but they were for my funeral.

-it's too late to save me now

you left without a note. that is
why i always search for you
through poetry,

hoping that i might somehow
find you in the next few lines.

-the words you never said

23

i'm seated in a room filled with
people i know. it's already past
midnight and i have mentally
counted everyone around me
for the thousandth time.

it just never stops, no matter
how much i want it to.

-obsessive-compulsive disorder

i still remember the time when i first
started feeling a little *crazy*. i had just
turned seventeen and was suddenly
infatuated with the idea of taking my
own life.

i used to come home after school, lie
face down on my bed, and think about
it repeatedly without any reason. and
then i'd just cry profusely. it soon
turned into a habit as i slowly began
planning the *ending*—completely
unaware of what was happening to me.

because each step of the way felt
satisfying, even if it was the thought
of me dying.

-this is how my suicidal thoughts started

the value of happiness,
only a sad person knows.

the scent of a flower,
yearned only by someone
who has lost the sense of
smell.

the meaning of love,
understood only after going
through a heartbreak.

the importance of winds,
appreciated only when the
kites cannot be flown.

the power of dreaming,
reflected only when one is
overwhelmed by failure.

the ones who truly care,
revealed only when the
journey gets tough.

the essence of freedom,
valued only when one is
in captivity.

the importance of life,
realized only after you've
tried ending it.

-the meaning of everything good

"what makes you hate yourself so much?"
echoed a familiar voice. *"is it because
of all the suffering that you go through?"*

"no. not at all. it's the little moments
of happiness that scare me. because
they give birth to the idea that life
can be good to you; that life isn't so
miserable after all, when i know so
well that there is no truth to it."

-hating joy

i felt happy yesterday—for a
moment at least. but then it
started to feel a little too
lonely.

so i had to search for all the
pieces of sadness and plead
with them to never abandon
me again.

-and they listened

when you first held my hands, my
only wish was for the moment to
be paused in time forever, so that
it was the only thing i experienced.

but if that were to come true, i'd
never get to know what night truly
felt like.

-darkness, my only friend

29

you asked me if i was
doing alright. i blankly
looked at you, smiled,
and faintly whispered:
"i'm fine."

silly me!

still hoping that you'd
somehow catch me
lying.

-a beautiful truth

in my first heartbreak, i cried
abundantly. but over time, i
found myself complaining each
time someone broke my heart—

because it no longer hurt like it
once did.

-*some things we just got used to*

31

yesterday, i wrote a few lines of
poetry but had to erase them
afterward because there wasn't
much depth to it.

so today, i cut myself again.

-this is how poetry started

32

i wrote a myriad of journal entries
when i turned seventeen.

some were about how my day went,
while the rest were beautifully riddled
with the thought of just ending my
life.

-the inception

33

i do not know why, but
the thought of just ending
my life gives me immense
satisfaction.

-a beautiful compulsion

34

my psychiatrist prescribed me
some 'happy' pills each time i
went for my review. and when
i told her that i had become
more suicidal as a result of
them,

all she did was give me more.

-the pretty little side effects

35

you asked me why i loved
darkness so much. what
could i say?

we become fond of the
things that never leave.

-a companion

36

if ever i fail to make it,
please know that i've
suffered too much and
have had too little to
lean on.

i'm sorry.

-suicide note

37

they cry when you
are dead but nobody
shows up to comfort
when you are crying.

-the society we live in

you told me that everything
would get better with time.

and surely it did.

i just wasn't there to see it.

-when i'm gone

the first pill i took didn't
do much. but the last one
made me a little drowsy.

what i had forgotten was
that in between, i took a
dozen of them.

-why do i do these things?

they gave me a 'mood stabilizer',
doubled the dosage in just two
months, and then asked me how
i felt.

-a walking zombie

41

i went to the gardens where
we last met and saw that all
the flowers had vanished.

and then i realized: you left
and took all the fragrance
with you.

-*sometimes it hurts*

42

i wrote your name right next
to mine in a piece of patterned
paper and submerged it in water.
after a while, i took it out and
saw that one of the names had
faded.

and it was not yours.

-losing myself

43

i wish i had been born
different.

in that way, i'd perhaps
feel pain differently.

-somethings are just meant to be

when you left, i lamented with tears
on the first day. then on the second,
third, and the fourth. over time, my
only cradle of healing was through
weeping.

that is why i still cry so much today.

-you asked me why my eyes were always sore

45

suddenly, all of my wishes
came true. that is why i
continued feeling sad.

-you thought i'd wish for happiness

my psychiatrist asked me if i
had started feeling any better,
after three months on the pill.
i instantly replied: yes.

i was now more happy about
ending my life.

-the side effect no one talks about

47

each time i feel happy, i come
to the grim realization that at
this moment in time, i could
just be as sad.

in a thousand different ways.

-this is my happiness-to-sadness ratio

if one doesn't work, they prescribe
the other. if the other doesn't work,
they prescribe both. if both do not
work, they increase the dosage. and
if it still doesn't work, they put you
under care.

and once you've lost every sense of
self-awareness:

then you're 'cured'.

-a beautiful psychiatry story

49

you wanted to be loved
and i did too. but only
one of us could give in
return.

-unrequited love

panadol for the sick and
prozac for the *'sick'* as well.

but the one difference:

only the former cured.

-the not-so-magical pills

51

i stood next to the river and wept
uncontrollably. the shimmering
cascades of tears mixed with water
and gave life to the flowers nearby.

after a week, i picked a few of them
and placed them beside my pillows.

in return, it prevented the next tear
from falling.

-the grand scheme of things

52

in between all my sorrow,
there are glimpses of joy
during which i smile a little.

and then go back to crying.

-unbreakable habits

53

you say that you love poetry.
there is a piece i wrote which
i'd really want you to read.

only when i'm not around.

-suicide note

and in the end, my love:

the things that make us
happy are the same things
that will swallow us with
sadness.

-*laws of nature*

55

my dreams were frequently
about *happiness*.

but one night, it just felt a
bit too real that i forgot to
wake up the next day.

-the end of pain

the waves craved my sight all
evening. because they knew that i
always sat next to them and sang
harmoniously.

but this time, they did not realize
that i had become a part of them.

-a beautiful suicide story

57

you wrote a few lines and asked
my heart to complete the rest.
what my heart didn't know was
that it would irrecoverably fall
for the little you had penned.

and in the process, forget that
it even mattered.

-lost myself loving you

the flower got all the light it
needed. but then it realized:

it needed darkness to bloom.

-never forget

59

i wept uncontrollably. and waited
for you to come and tell me that
everything was going to be alright.
but you insisted that you did not
hear me cry because it had been
raining heavily outside.

o love:

it wasn't *rain* you heard.

-the sounds of my tears

the cracks in me have started
to leak again. and no amount
of bandages can save me this
time.

-a broken mind

61

i knew so little about happiness.

so it never occurred to me that
it was something i could have.

-the reason you don't see me smiling

i quickly wiped my tears as i
saw you approaching from a
distance. because i knew that
you'd give me fresher, more
desperate ones.

and i didn't want you to think
that other things too could
make me cry.

-i love the way you make me weep

63

my idea of happiness is wrapped
in the idea of hating myself just a
little less compared to yesterday.

and it works pretty well.

-why do you hate yourself so much?

each day, i wake up and
think of ways in which
i can be sad differently.

-it's meant to be

65

just like the moon, if you came any
closer, there would be mayhem. and
if you went any further, the tide of
affection between us would weaken.

just at a distance is what has kept
everything in harmony.

-attachments

in my first session, my psychiatrist
prescribed me twenty milligrams
of prozac.

while the rest of the appointments
were her continuously asking if i
had become any happier.

-how could i disappoint her?

this suicidal mind will end
up taking my life or continue
leaving me with just a little
less of it each new day. but
what's scary is that the first
one doesn't even bother me
anymore.

it's the latter where i'd still
live to feel everything.

all over again.

-things we just get used to

the flowers pleaded for water,
so i gave it to them. but they
let their thorns have it first.

because that way, the scent
would be much stronger.

-embracing our chaotic side first

69

in all essence, love can never
be truly complete without
heartbreak.

-you asked me why i was broken

i stared at the person right
in front of the mirror and
felt nothing.

the person looking back
felt everything it seemed.

-this is bipolar

71

the vase fell five feet to the
ground and remained the
same.

it then looked at me and
faintly whispered: *it's only
you who's broken.*

-someone had to

i regret the many times i held back my
tears. because in all essence, they are the
ones who truly embraced me when no
one else would; they acted as cushions
during each frantic fall; they showed
genuine comfort when everything else
became intolerable; they helped without
judgment.

they became the only source of light
when even the sun was mad at me; they
sang graciously when all other music
had stopped; they put out every little
flame, even when everyone else wanted
to see the world burn; they brought me
to poetry when everything else looked
chaotic.

and they carried me to safety when
every other thought wanted me dead.

-dearest tears

73

i wish i had met you earlier.
that way, i'd perhaps get to
hold your hands a little bit
longer—

even if it was just by a minute.

-i miss you so much

someone else is staring at
the same secluded star as
you are right now, but with
a different thought in mind.

maybe happier.

-your turn will also come

75

the happiest of the emotions
may have already been felt
long ago.

that is why there is so much
poetry about the little that is
remaining.

-when your sunshine is gone

my therapist asked me why i wanted
to end my life. i looked blankly at her
and suddenly started questioning
everything before me.

because in all reality, i could not think
of any reason.

-and yet, that's all i could think about

77

everyone looked away when i was falling.
but when i somehow managed to pull
myself together, they blamed me for
being too blind.

-the society we live in

to live is to die every day;
to die is to stop living.

and life is truly lived only
when one is not afraid of
dying.

-a life's tale

79

the raindrops graciously
fell on top of me.

in return, i stood there
apologizing for being in
its intended path.

-sorry for all the little things

there is a liking i have developed
for a tree right next to my room,
thinking how the branches would
beautifully support my lifeless
body.

-*the truest account of my thoughts*

the way you left me no longer
hurts.

it's the way you loved me that
still gives me the greatest, most
agonizing pain.

-o love, why did you leave?

i gently laced the blue belt around my
neck, attached it to the nail on the slightly
discolored wall—about the same height as
myself—and suspended from it: thought
by thought, centimeter by centimeter.

the seconds passed by unhurriedly. i could
feel the fine leather pressing tightly against
my skin as i slowly started losing consciousness.
my veins surged with heat, then froze, as if
winter crept through them. i felt my heartbeat
fade a little, a fragile pulse, growing frantic
with every weakening thud. it was like being
submerged in the deepest of the oceans. but
here, i could escape. and yet, i added more
weight to my body. and when i could no
longer bear the pain, i impassively got up.

what's worse is that even after knowing
what it feels like, i still think of doing that
again.

-suicide

83

the flowers that lay on top of
my body wept uncontrollably.

no one knew—

i had planted and watered
them.

-the cycle of life

84

i talked, i paused, and i listened.

but what you didn't realize was
that i had repeatedly counted
you and everyone around you
inside my head.

-ocd

85

i asked for happiness, and that
was all i got, even if it was the
littlest bit of it.

i asked for misery, and it made
me realize that it was never
about happiness in the first
place.

-a thousand reasons to cry

i'd count myself lucky if i
somehow made it to the
psych ward.

otherwise, this raw mind
is trying arduously to pull
me closer to death.

-please help me

87

i'd sometimes lie quietly on my
bed and contemplate ending my
life, just to envisage everyone
who would show up and cry
at my funeral.

and then i'd cry profusely.

-reasons to weep

it's a battle every single day:

should i hang myself right
now or should i wait for
another day just to feel
the same?

-somethings are meant to be

once, the heart knew
nothing of heartbreak.

and then, it was the
only thing it could feel.

-a hearts tale

there is a funeral at home.

and suddenly, i feel very
important.

-no one to wipe a tear when you're suffering

91

the beauty of a flower:

even after being plucked and
faced with imminent death, it
still puts a smile on the same
face that led to this.

-remember that

yogesh chandra

i have never wished
for happiness, my love.

just a little less misery
would suffice.

-some sunshine for the sad soul

93

i looked at you and found all
my reasons to live,

oblivious to the idea that one
day, you'd be the reason why
it ended.

-love is suicidal

and when i was gone, they
wondered why i hadn't left
a note.

how could i tell them? you
mistook all my words for
poetry all this while.

-a big beautiful suicide note

95

i've always wondered what
happiness felt like. even
during the times i was *happy*.

-*when you've only known misery*

in its truest and rawest form:

the thought of my neck suddenly
snapping as gravity slowly pulls
me down makes me downright
happy.

-call me crazy

97

i expressed all the words
you always wanted to hear.

in return, you whispered
everything that you had
once promised never to
utter.

-heartbreak

i have always searched for you
through poetry.

if it's destiny, then maybe it'll
be the last few where i'll get
to find and hold you.

-you promised you'd never leave

i always lose to the night,
because it sees light faster
than i ever did,

even if we joined a thousand
different nights.

-the endless darkness

you asked for the directions to
home, and i did too. you managed
to reach on time, and i did too.

the only difference was that your
idea of *home* was not the same as
mine.

-i want to sleep forever

a thousand reasons to live
in a thousand different
ways.

yet here we are, searching
for that one reason every
dawn, which ends our lives
in a thousand different
ways.

-the depressed mind

yogesh chandra

every diary entry once had
me writing about you.

and now, every suicide note
has me writing of you.

[happiness]

-the irony

the flowers saw me at my lowest,
and you did too. it was perhaps
a coincidence when you put the
same flowers over my lifeless
body,

wishing that you had reached
out to me earlier.

-contemporary art

everyone had the same song in
front of them, but it was all
sung differently.

everyone had the same reasons
to be happy about, but it was
all felt differently.

everyone had different reasons
to be sad about, but life ended
in the same way.

-suicide

i begged the moon not
to leave me in darkness.
the moon begged the sun
for nothing different.

and ironically, the sun
begged me not to come
any closer.

-the light we so selfishly desire

the eyes could only do so little,
my love.

we look at everyone around us,
but can never truly see them.

-the battles within

107

the littlest of the mistakes we
made as teenagers turned out
to be the biggest of the lessons
we've learned as adults.

-young love

everything that you'll feel
tomorrow has already been
felt by someone before you.

-never forget

it was a blissful black night. i quietly
penned my thoughts on a sheet of
scented grey paper, folded it gently,
and placed it right next to me. then
i went to bed.

when i failed to open my eyes the
next day, you curiously read the
beautifully apt note.

but what's tragic is that once you
had finished reading, you had to
assume i was *happy*.

-coincidentally, some days i write about happiness

you searched for me under the
rare blue moon, hoping you'd
somehow get a glimpse.

i wish you knew:

you'd only find me inside the
eye of the storm.

-the art of misery

all of poetry is you. and
all of you is pain.

and if poetry is meant to
be this painful, i'd still
write about you forever.

-the love i could never have

the night knew so little
about light, so it had to
befriend the moon,

even after knowing that
it would be gone after
some time.

-the things we do for happiness

i searched for happiness in
every little place i possibly
could.

and while doing so, i
became more miserable.

-the paradox of happiness

please help me—
someone, anyone.

-words i quietly utter to myself every night

dear reader

with everything around you becoming so overwhelming, you seem
to have mastered the art of constantly hating yourself for being like
this. after all, why does it only have to happen to you? why is grief
so abundant and happiness so rare? why did you have to endure
heartbreak from the one person with whom you had planned your
entire future?

life is unfair in a thousand ways. some get to realize this earlier
while others spend a lifetime. the depressed get more reasons to
become downhearted, while the happy ones sit and wonder: what
is *'wrong'* with you? every new day seems to be a test: to continue
suffering or to put an end to it. i know what it feels like, each step
of the way. the mind is stuck in this desperate loop from which it
seems impossible to just snap out of. you may feel as if all the
doors have been permanently shut, that sunlight reaches everyone
but you, and that rainbows turn dark as soon as you look up at the
sky.

if this is your reality, you are not alone. some of us have been *gifted*
with this suffering in order to create some meaning out of life.
after all, we would never know the true value of happiness if we
did not get to experience sadness. and to the faintly beating heart
that has only known disloyalty: i see you, i feel you. to the grief-
stricken mind that is supported by a range of white and green
coated pills: there is sunshine at the end. just hold on for one more
day. and then, another...

this book should have been out last year, but it simply could not happen. i had spent, for the most part, battling the very demons i thought had gone away. for a moment, i had started feeling those butterflies all over again. i felt happy with her; i felt valued; i felt special. she made me feel at home and promised that she'd never leave. but like all times, *happiness* was just short-lived. i desperately pleaded with her; i uncontrollably cried in front of her on my birthday, begging her a thousand times not to leave me like this. but it wasn't meant to be.

i had to withdraw in my shell and was pushed into the deepest state of depression. every morning started with thoughts of her, every afternoon was spent replaying her memories on repeat, and every night was consumed by endless sobbing. i simply could not let go. and so, my only companion in thought held my hands once again: i had to somehow end my life. the compulsion was back, but this time, it only had fatal intentions. in my last cries for help, i went to the therapist, took pills to make me feel good, and called her for two straight months, begging her repeatedly to take me back.

and when i had lost all sense of hope, i bought a thick white rope from a store nearby and kept it close to me. each night, when the pain got unbearable, i'd tie it around my neck and pull the opposite ends as tightly as i could, just to suffocate myself. i wanted to experience how dying felt. this continued for days, with the pull getting stronger each new time. and soon, i'd attach the rope to the wall, at about the same height as myself, and slowly let gravity pull me down. in those desperate moments, dying felt good. and so, i had finally decided to *do it*. to a tree right next to my home, i made a knot on the rope, put it around my neck, and securely tied the other end to a branch about three meters above the ground. all i had to do now was jump.

till today, i still don't know what made me change my mind in the dying seconds. this is the book i have written afterward. please be gentle.

about the writer

yogesh chandra is a poet based in fiji. he found therapy in poetry and engages with the audience on topics relating to depression, suicide, grief, and healing. he draws inspiration from the chaos that he had been presented with right from childhood. he shares his writings with the world to raise awareness on mental illness and aspires to be a voice for those who suffer in silence. when he is not writing, yogesh loves to explore the natural surroundings around him. he also pursues landscape photography as a hobby. his photography, including his blogs and poetry, can be viewed on his website at:

https://writerscornerfiji.wixsite.com/poetryandfiction

www.ingramcontent.com/pod-product-compliance
Lightning Source LLC
Chambersburg PA
CBHW020734160726

47993CB00006B/2442